Coloring book for adults and kids amazing cocking image for design

This coloring book is belongs to

____

____

____

KITCHEN
MILK
I can COOKING!
F

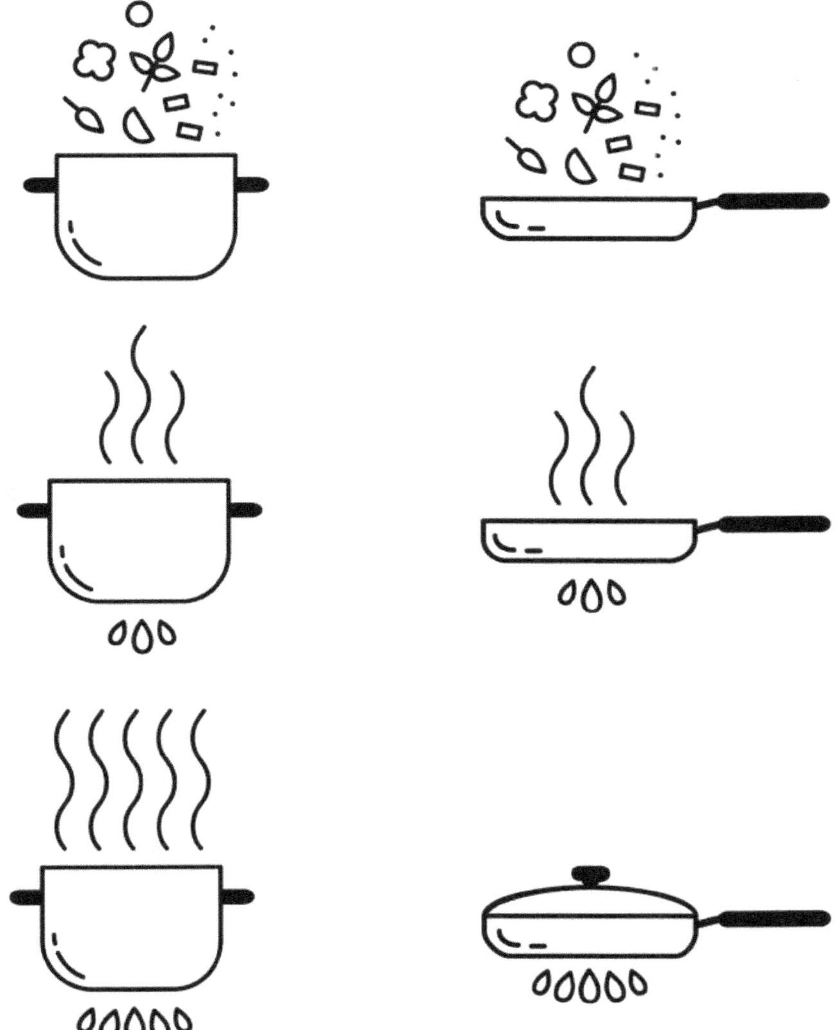

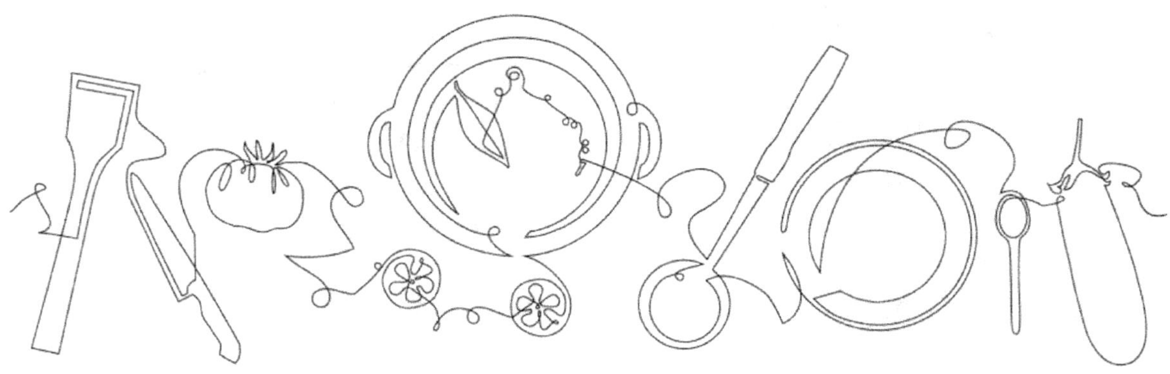

Let's
COOK
together

Restaurant
CLASSIC RECIPES

Love
COOK
ing

COOk
ing

Menu

Cooking
premium

mix taste stir
lemons
1cup
YEAST
oz.
25 min.
glass
tbs.
ts.
FLOUR
1/2 1/3 1/4 2/3
salted
pound baking unsalted
sugar bake at butter
ADD Pinch of
salt soda

INGREDIENTS
MIX

Juice

FLOUR
SUGAR
American cuisine
PANCAKE WITH STRAWBERRY AND BANANA

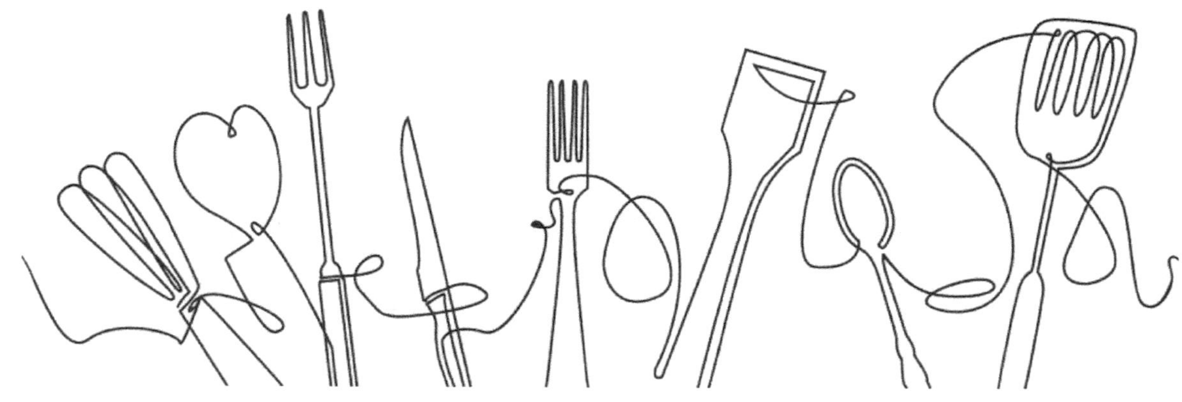

FLOUR
SUGAR
American cuisine
PANCAKE WITH STRAWBERRY AND BANANA

cooking equipment
BAKING STUFF
useful things
SUGAR
VANILLA SUGAR
MILK
BAKING SODA

COOKING

MILK
I love
BAKING
VANILLA SUGAR
SUGAR
BAKING SODA

HOW TO COOK PORRIDGE

LEMON PIE
EGGS
LEMONS
LEMON ZEST
FLOUR
FLOUR
BUTTER
SUGAR
BAKING SODA
MILK
ADD
MIX
SALT
BAKE
APPLES

Let's
COOK
together

Restaurant
CLASSIC RECIPES

Love
COOK
ing

COOK
ing

Menu

Cooking
premium

LOVE
Cooking.
Recipe

Chocolate Cake

SIMPLE RECIPE

Kitchen

TEA & DESSERT

March

CALENDAR SET
sketch and calligraphy

Chocolate Cake
SIMPLE RECIPE

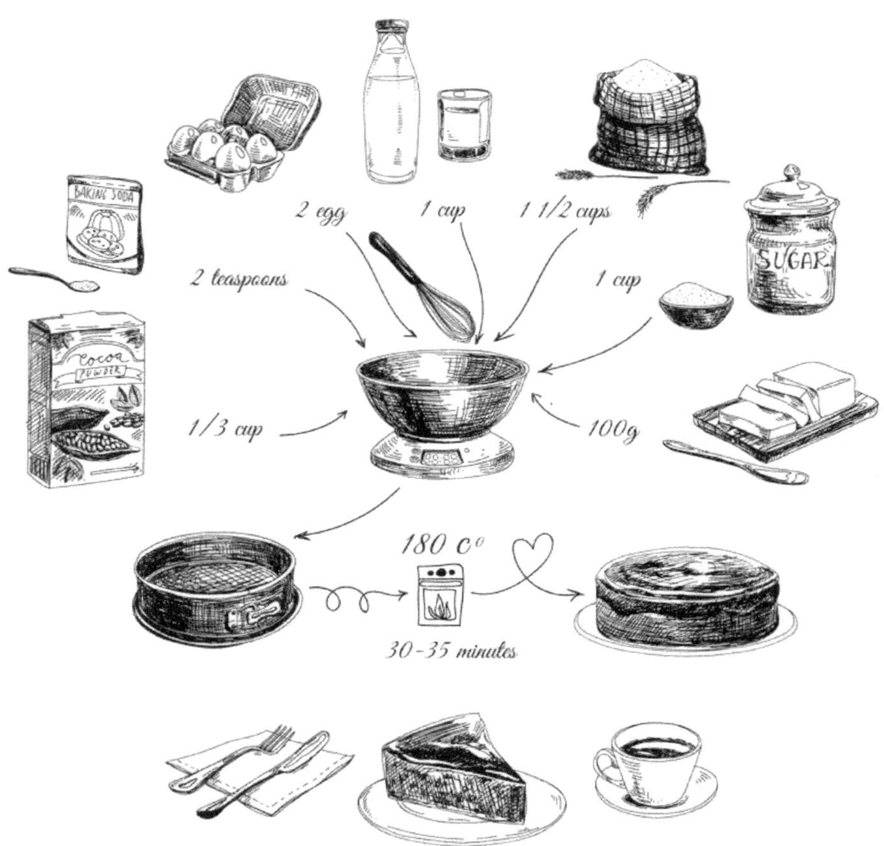

Lemon Pound Cake

SIMPLE RECIPE

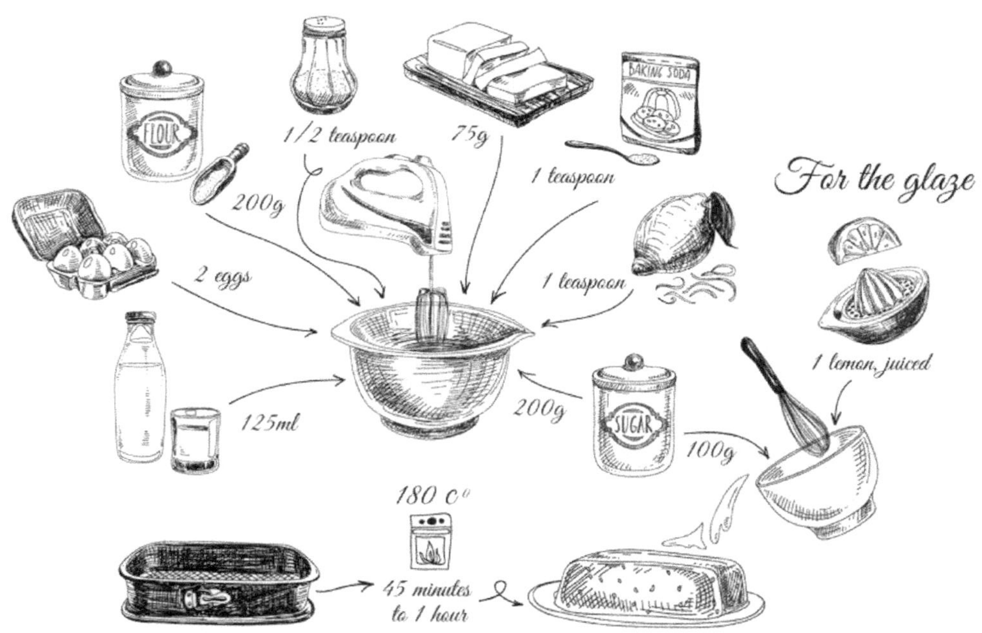

pumpkin Soup recipe
thyme
onion garlic
carrot pepper cut
cream water
ginger salt mush
seeds

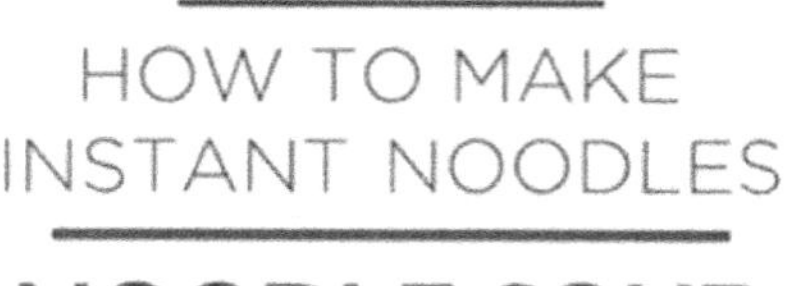

HOW TO MAKE
INSTANT NOODLES
NOODLE SOUP

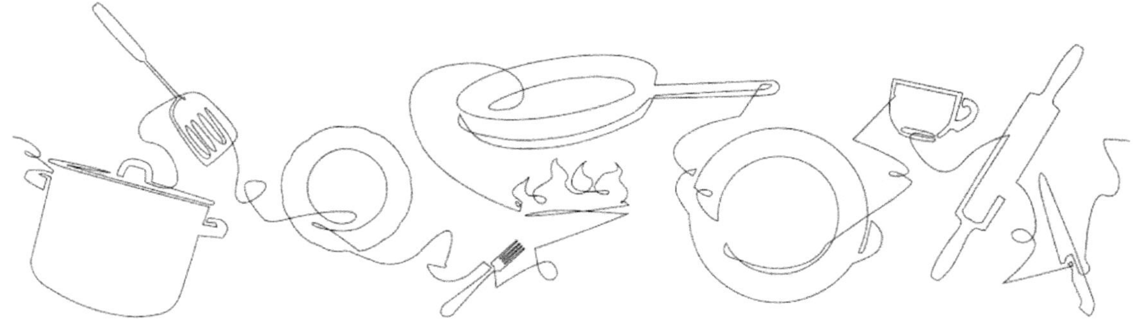

HIGH-TEA

Baked
With
Love

HeALTH
CARE

Fresh
Bread

Food
RECIPE
COOKING
WHIPPING
CREAM
VINEGAR
2 l

~Doodle Food Set~